DATE DUE

MR 30'92			
JE 1'92			
AR 14 '95			
JUN 17 95			
FEB 13 '97			
JUN 29			
DE 13 99			
02-11-07			
DE 04 12			

Smoking

Distinguishing Between Fact and Opinion

Curriculum Consultant: JoAnne Buggey, Ph.D.
College of Education, University of Minnesota

By Bonnie Szumski

OPPOSING
JUNIORS
VIEWPOINTS®

90069

Greenhaven Press, Inc.
Post Office Box 289009
San Diego, CA 92128-9009

Titles in the opposing viewpoints juniors series:

Smoking	Death Penalty
Gun Control	Drugs and Sports
Animal Rights	Toxic Wastes
AIDS	Patriotism
Alcohol	Working Mothers
Immigration	Terrorism

Library of Congress Cataloging-in-Publication Data

Smoking : distinguishing between fact and opinion / [edited] by Bonnie
    Szumski ; curriculum consultant, JoAnne Buggey.
        p.   cm. — (Opposing viewpoints juniors)
    Summary: Presents opposing viewpoints on such aspects of
smoking as the possible harmful effects of passive smoking, cigarette
advertising, and the role of common courtesy in the smoking debate.
    ISBN 0-89908-469-9
    1. Tobacco habit—United States—Juvenile literature. 2. Smoking—
United States—Juvenile literature.   [1. Smoking.] I. Szumski,
Bonnie, 1958- .   II. Series.
HV5735.S67 1989
613.85—dc20   89-2153
                                                                        CIP
                                                                        AC

CONTENTS

An Introduction to Opposing Viewpoints

When people disagree, it is hard to figure out who is right. You may decide one person is right just because the person is your friend or relative. But this is not a very good reason to agree or disagree with someone. It is better if you try to understand why these people disagree. On what main points do the two people disagree? Read or listen to each person's argument carefully. Separate the facts and opinions that each person presents. Finally, decide which argument best matches what you think. This process, examining an argument without emotion, is part of what critical thinking is all about.

This is not easy. Many things make it hard to understand and form opinions. People's values, age, and experience all influence the way they think. This is why learning to read and think critically is an invaluable skill. Opposing Viewpoints Juniors books will help you learn and practice skills to improve your ability to read critically. By reading opposing views on an issue, you will become familiar with methods people use to attempt to convince you that their point of view is right. And you will learn to separate the authors' opinions from the facts they present.

Each Opposing Viewpoints Juniors book focuses on one critical thinking skill that will help you judge the views presented. Some of these skills are telling fact from opinion, recognizing propaganda techniques, and locating and analyzing the main idea. These skills will allow you to examine opposing viewpoints more easily. Each viewpoint is paraphrased from the original to make it easier to read. The viewpoints are placed in a running debate and are always placed with the pro view first.

What Is the Difference Between Fact and Opinion?

In this Opposing Viewpoints Juniors book you will be asked to identify and study statements of fact and statements of opinion. A fact is a statement that can be proved true. Here are some examples of factual statements: "The Statue of Liberty was dedicated in 1886 in New York," "Dinosaurs are extinct," and "George Washington was the first U.S. President." It is a fairly easy thing to prove these facts true. For instance, a historian in the year 3000 might need to prove when the Statue of Liberty was dedicated. One way she might do this is to check in the Hall of Records in New York. She would try to find a source to verify the date. Sometimes it is harder to prove facts true. And some ideas that are stated as facts may not be. In this book you will be asked to question facts presented in the viewpoints and be given some ways in which you might go about proving them.

Statements of opinion cannot be proved. An opinion is a statement that expresses how a person feels about something or what a person thinks is true. Remember the facts we mentioned? They can easily be changed into statements of opinion. For example, "Dinosaurs became extinct because a huge meteor hit the Earth," "George Washington was the best president the United States ever had," and "Rebuilding the Statue of Liberty was a waste of money," are all statements of opinion. They express what one person believes to be true. Opinions are not better than facts. They are different. Opinions are based on many things, including religious, social, moral, and family values. Opinions can also be based on medical and scientific facts. For instance, many scientists have made intelligent guesses about other planets based on what they know is true about Earth. The only way these scientists would know their opinions were right is if they were able to visit other planets and test their guesses. Until their guesses are proved, then, they remain opinions. Some people have opinions that we do not like, or with which we disagree. That does not always make their opinions wrong, or right. There is room in our world for many different opinions.

When you read differing views on any issue, it is very important to know when people are using facts and when they are using opinions in an argument. When writers use facts, it makes their argument more believable and easier to prove. The more facts the author has, the more the reader can tell that the writer's opinion is based on something other than personal feelings.

Authors that base their arguments mostly on their own opinions, then, are impossible to prove factually true.

This does not mean that these types of argument are not as meaningful. It means that you, as the reader, must decide whether or not you agree or disagree based on personal reasons, not factual ones.

We asked two students to give their opinions on the smoking issue. Examine the following viewpoints. Look for facts and opinions in their arguments.

I believe smoking is dangerous and stupid.

It's been proven that smoking cigarettes causes cancer. The Surgeon General of the United States believes it. He's the one who made the rule that tobacco companies have to put warnings on cigarette packages that say how dangerous smoking is. Plus, there have been dozens of government reports and animal studies to prove that people who smoke are at a higher risk of having lung cancer and emphysema.

I think it's dumb when kids smoke to look older because they're just going to get sick and hurt their health. Plus, it smells bad and looks gross.

Also, my friend's dad has lung cancer, and he smokes. The doctor told him that his smoking is what caused the lung cancer. Isn't that proof enough?

I don't think there's anything wrong with smoking.

I don't understand what the big deal is about smoking. People are always saying how bad it is for you, but my grandfather is about 60. He smokes and he's healthy.

The way I figure it is, if you enjoy it you should be able to smoke if you want to. Nobody knows for sure if smoking can hurt you or not.

I know a lot of smokers. They say smoking can help you relax. Also, it's fun to smoke with your friends. If they're all having a cigarette, it's hard not to want one. Plus, let's face it, smoking looks great.

Sure, some people *say* they got sick from smoking, and maybe they did. But that doesn't mean *everyone* who smokes will get sick. So why do people have to get on smokers' backs about it? People should just let smokers smoke if they want to. After all, smokers aren't hurting anyone.

If someone wanted to know which side you were on, who would you agree with? Why?

ANALYZING THE
SAMPLE VIEWPOINTS

Chris and Natasha have very different opinions about smoking. Both of them use examples of fact and opinion in their arguments:

Chris:

FACTS

the surgeon general's warning is on cigarette packages

studies have been done that link cigarettes to disease

OPINIONS

smoking smells bad

looks gross

Natasha:

FACTS

grandfather smokes and is healthy

not everyone who smokes gets cancer

OPINIONS

it's nice to smoke with friends

smoking helps you relax

In this sample, Chris and Natasha both have an equal number of facts and opinions. Chris's facts are based on the opinions of authorities. Natasha's facts, on the other hand, are based on personal experience. Both Chris and Natasha think that they are right about smoking. What conclusions would you come to from this sample? Why? Think of two facts and two opinions that you have about smoking. As you continue to read through the viewpoints in this book, try keeping a tally like the one above to compare the authors' arguments.

CHAPTER 1

PREFACE: Is Passive Smoking Harmful to the Nonsmoker?

Most people agree that smoking causes some negative health effects. But there is widespread disagreement over the harmfulness of passive smoking. Can someone get lung disease by simply inhaling another person's cigarette smoke?

In the next two viewpoints, the authors debate this question. Each author's conclusions lead to a different view of the future. The first author concludes that if passive smoking is harmful to the nonsmoker, then society should enforce laws that restrict smoking in public places. The second author concludes that if evidence for harm from second-hand smoke is not very strong, and he believes it is not, these laws are unnecessary and harmful.

When reading these two viewpoints, use your skills to find the facts and opinions each author presents. Which case is more strongly based on fact, or are they equally factual?

Passive smoking is harmful to the nonsmoker

Editor's Note: This viewpoint is paraphrased from an article by C. Everett Koop, the Surgeon General of the United States. Dr. Koop's office released a report in 1986 that concluded that passive smoking is harmful to nonsmokers. When reading this viewpoint, and the next, pay close attention to the facts the authors use.

What is Dr. Koop's definition of a smoke-free society? Does it sound possible?

On what evidence does the author base his conclusions? Is this evidence factual?

I first called for a "smoke-free society" by the year 2000 three years ago. What I meant was a society in which nobody would smoke in the presence of others without permission. I feel sure that this kind of society can be achieved.

We have known smoking to be a killer since the first Surgeon General's report in 1964. In the United States, it is the cause of at least 360,000 deaths each year—that is the same as a packed jumbo jet crashing every 12 hours. Smoking is the direct cause of heart attacks, emphysema, and lung cancer. It is now the leading preventable cause of death.

How harmful is it to inhale other people's cigarette smoke? While there is much still to be learned about its effects, my position is this: scientific studies have shown enough proof to justify my calling this smoke a health hazard.

"I'VE SMOKED ALL MY LIFE, AND IT NEVER HURT ME!"

Doug Marlette, reprinted with permission.

My report was based on the work of more than 60 scientists. These scientists came to the conclusion that involuntary smoking is a cause of disease, including lung cancer, in healthy nonsmokers.

Another study has also confirmed that exposure to other people's smoke increases the risk of the nonsmoker getting lung cancer. The risk of lung cancer is about 30 percent higher for nonsmoking spouses of smokers than for nonsmoking spouses of nonsmokers.

Wheezing and coughing are increased about 20 to 80 percent in children of smokers. Infants of smokers are more likely to get pneumonia and bronchitis.

Another study conducted at the University of California at San Francisco studied 7000 nonsmoking women. This study found that nonsmoking wives of current smokers were more likely to suffer heart attacks than wives of men who did not smoke.

Robert Rosner of the Smoking Policy Institute was talking to a group of businessmen about restricting smoking in the workplace. First he frightened them with the health hazards. Then he shocked them with numbers—a smoker costs a company up to $5000 more a year than a nonsmoker. When he'd finished, one businessman said, "Mr. Rosner, you left out the main reason for creating a smoke-free environment."

"What's that?" Rosner asked.

"It should happen," the man said, "because it's right."

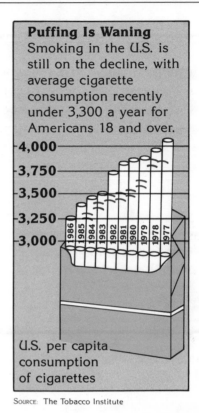

Puffing Is Waning
Smoking in the U.S. is still on the decline, with average cigarette consumption recently under 3,300 a year for Americans 18 and over.

U.S. per capita consumption of cigarettes

SOURCE: The Tobacco Institute

Is the author's conclusion a fact or an opinion? Do you agree or disagree?

Can nonsmokers get lung cancer from cigarettes?

Dr. Koop cites two studies other than his own report to support his argument that passive smoking causes lung cancer. What did these studies conclude? Do they support Dr. Koop's argument?

Editor's Note: This viewpoint was paraphrased from an article written by Thomas E. Smith Jr., a U.S. Senator from South Carolina. In it, he argues that nonsmokers are not harmed by passive smoking.

What are the facts the author uses to criticize the Japanese report?

Anti-smokers are using certain research reports to try and prove that nonsmokers are harmed by cigarette smoke.

A Japanese study found that nonsmoking wives of smokers have a higher risk for lung cancer than nonsmoking women married to nonsmokers. Anti-smokers quote this study even though it has been criticized.

Experts argued that the study did not take into account other kinds of household smoke, such as cooking smoke and indoor heating flames. Other factors that might affect health, like diet, family history, and job-related exposure, were also not counted.

Russell Myers, reprinted with permission: Tribune Media Services.

Some have claimed that some tobacco smoke fumes, like carbon monoxide and nicotine, are dangerous to nonsmokers' health. These claims overlook many scientific facts. Research has shown carbon monoxide is mainly produced by cars and industry. Indoor levels are affected by these outside levels, by cooking and heating, even by the number of people around. In spite of this, tobacco smoke is blamed for adding carbon monoxide to the body and endangering the health of nonsmokers.

Studies that are done under more realistic conditions show that the level of carbon monoxide from tobacco smoke is very small. Dr. Duncan Hutcheon confirms this: "Environmental studies suggest that tobacco smoke has little impact on the carbon monoxide content of room air."

Measurements of carbon monoxide really do not prove that tobacco smoke harms the nonsmoker. This is because so many other things, like cars and factories, produce it. Nicotine is a more reliable factor, and the studies that measure nicotine show that the effect of tobacco smoke on air quality is slight.

Drs. William Hinds and Melvin First found only very small amounts of nicotine in the air of bars, bus and airline terminals, and restaurants. Their study found that a nonsmoker would have to spend 100 hours in the smokiest bar to inhale as much smoke as in one filter-tip cigarette.

Thus it is clear that a lot of misinformation and numerous unproved theories have confused the nonsmoker health question. The claim that tobacco smoke causes disease in nonsmokers is simply not convincing.

What facts does the author use to support his point about carbon monoxide?

Why does the author think the level of nicotine is more important? What facts does he use in this paragraph?

Bogus studies?

Mr. Smith argues that the evidence that passive smoking is harmful is not convincing. He, like Dr. Koop, quotes from studies. What factors does Mr. Smith believe were not taken into account? How might you go about proving whether or not the studies cited by Mr. Smith were accurate or not?

Tallying the Facts and Opinions

After reading the two viewpoints on passive smoking, make a chart similar to the one made for Chris and Natasha on page 4. List the facts and opinions each author gives to make his case. A chart is started for you below:

Koop:

FACTS

360,000 deaths a year from smoking

OPINIONS

stopping people from smoking is right

Smith:

FACTS

study did not take into account household fumes

OPINIONS

the claim that passive smoking is harmful is not convincing

Which article used more factual statements? Which, did you think, was the most convincing? Why? Which one did you personally agree with? Why? List some facts and opinions, not in the articles, that have influenced your opinion.

CHAPTER 2

PREFACE: Should Cigarette Advertising Be Banned?

The authors of the next two viewpoints debate whether or not cigarette advertising should be banned. The viewpoints center on two issues. One issue is whether advertising is protected by the First Amendment. This is the amendment to the Constitution of the United States that protects every person's freedom of speech. Some people say that cigarette ads are protected by the First Amendment, and banning cigarette advertising would violate the tobacco companies' freedom of speech.

The other issue is whether a dangerous product should be advertised. Many believe cigarette companies should not be allowed to advertise because cigarettes have been proven to harm people's health. Cigarette ads make smoking look glamorous and exciting. Critics argue that this makes young people want to smoke. Banning these ads would, then, stop young people from smoking.

When reading these two viewpoints, pay attention to the authors' facts and opinions on this issue.

Cigarette advertising should be banned

Editor's Note: This viewpoint was paraphrased from an article written by The American Medical Association, one of the largest organizations of doctors in the country. In it, they argue that smoking is so dangerous that society must ban advertisements promoting it.

Do you think the authors' reasoning about an ad ban is fact or opinion? Why?

Are these facts or opinions? How might you go about proving these statements?

We, the American Medical Association, have called for a ban on all advertising and promotion of tobacco products for a very simple reason: Physicians cannot bear to watch their patients die from diseases that can be prevented.

Cigarettes are one of the most advertised products in the U.S.A. About 2 billion dollars is spent each year by domestic cigarette companies on advertising. Since radio and TV advertising of cigarettes was banned in 1971, cigarette companies have become the heaviest users of newspaper, magazine, and billboard advertising.

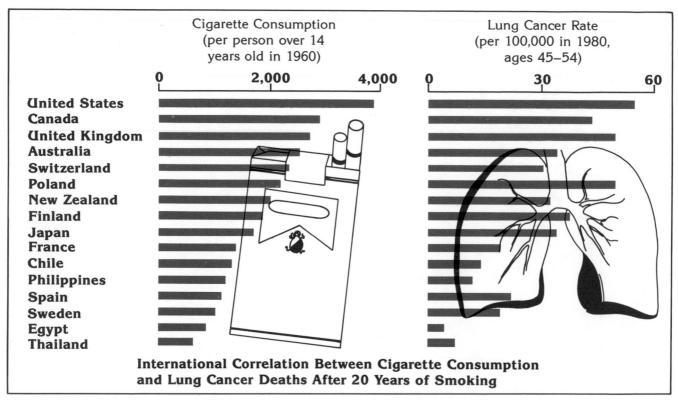

Cigarette Consumption
(per person over 14
years old in 1960)

Lung Cancer Rate
(per 100,000 in 1980,
ages 45–54)

0   2,000   4,000   0   30   60

United States
Canada
United Kingdom
Australia
Switzerland
Poland
New Zealand
Finland
Japan
France
Chile
Philippines
Spain
Sweden
Egypt
Thailand

International Correlation Between Cigarette Consumption and Lung Cancer Deaths After 20 Years of Smoking

Source: U.S. Department of Agriculture   Source: World Health Organization

Cigarette ads make smoking look socially acceptable. They are especially appealing to children and adolescents who want to be adults. They depict the "good life"—images of smokers enjoying good health, youthful vigor, and social and professional success.

Because tobacco is a dangerous product, a government ban on tobacco advertising and promotion would not harm the First Amendment. It was designed to protect the editorial freedom of the press and the right to religious, political, artistic, and scientific expression. It was not designed to protect companies' ability to advertise dangerous products.

We have been asked why we do not call for a ban on the sale of tobacco products. This country has learned from its experience with alcoholic beverages that prohibition just does not work. But education does work.

We will work to educate people about the health hazards of tobacco, including chewing tobacco and snuff. We will work to persuade people that tobacco is socially unacceptable. Stopping our citizens from being bombarded with the seductive messages of the tobacco companies will help our efforts.

Do you think the authors' argument about teens and smoking is fact or opinion? Do you think teens are attracted to smoking because of cigarette ads?

The authors argue that advertising is not protected by the First Amendment. Is this a fact or an opinion?

Bloom County by Berke Breathed

Berke Breathed © 1987, Washington Post Writers Group. Reprinted with permission.

How powerful is advertising?

List three facts and three opinions the authors give to prove their view that cigarette advertising is harmful.

What "simple reason" does the AMA give to tell us cigarette advertising should be banned? Do you agree with the authors that advertising makes people want to buy the product? Have you ever bought a product because of the way it was advertised? Did the product do what it was supposed to do?

Cigarette advertising should not be banned

Editor's Note: This viewpoint was paraphrased from an article written by Ira Glasser, who is the executive director of the American Civil Liberties Union, an organization that works to protect individuals' constitutional rights. Mr. Glasser argues that banning cigarette ads would violate cigarette companies' rights and would not stop people from smoking.

The author says that banning cigarette ads will lead to other free speech bans. Does he present any reasons why he thinks this?

I do not smoke, never have. Neither do any of my children, for which I am grateful. I know that nicotine is very addictive, and I believe that smoking is dangerous. But I am against bans on cigarette advertising, for two reasons.

First, censorship is a contagious disease. Many people who support the First Amendment believe that it would be possible to ban cigarette ads without affecting other First Amendment rights. I think they are fooling themselves, and us. They offer two arguments in defense of banning cigarette ads. One, the First Amendment does not apply to advertising as much as to political or artistic speech. Two, the fact that tobacco is so dangerous justifies banning its advertisements.

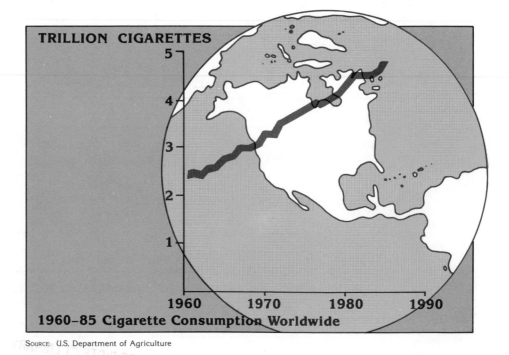

TRILLION CIGARETTES

1960–85 Cigarette Consumption Worldwide

Source: U.S. Department of Agriculture

If those two reasons actually worked to ban cigarette advertising, what might we expect? Once danger becomes a factor in restricting freedom of speech, the only important question is, Who defines what is dangerous? We do not want courts deciding what speech is too dangerous for us to hear.

My second reason for opposing bans is that there is little, if any, evidence that bans on cigarette advertising will reduce the number of Americans who smoke. In 1965, 43 percent of the adult population smoked; today, it is down to 30 percent. That is the largest reported decline for any widely-used addictive drug in the United States. Cigarette smoking began to fall off in the early 1970s, when health warnings first appeared on all cigarette ads and packages. It decreased again after the Federal Communications Commission required broadcasters to air anti-smoking replies to cigarette ads. Indeed, much of the decline in smoking occurred before cigarette ads were banned on television. In fact, cigarette smoking increased again right after the ban, probably because anti-smoking replies decreased. Over the past ten years, the percentage of adults who smoke has continued to drop, almost certainly as a result of public education.

In a fair contest between medical facts and the tobacco industry's self-serving propaganda, the facts will win. That is the reasoning behind the First Amendment. More public education is what we need, not bans on speech. If the government really wanted to show cigarette smoking as a danger, it would do away with the programs to support tobacco crops and fund a major national public education campaign, particularly aimed at children, on the harmfulness of smoking.

> The author is using a type of argument called "slippery slope"—which means if one thing happens, something worse will, too.

> What facts does the author use in this paragraph? What is his point?

> Do you think the author is right, that the "facts" will win? Can you name one situation where they might not win?

Is more education necessary?

List three facts and three opinions the author gives to prove his view that cigarette advertising is not harmful.

What are the two reasons the author presents in claiming cigarette ads should not be banned?

The author believes that people who are made aware of the dangers of smoking will not be influenced by cigarette ads. He argues that only people who are uneducated would smoke. Do you agree with the author that advertising does not influence people?

Analyzing Cigarette Advertising

Each one of us sees and hears dozens of advertising messages every day. Many of these ads also attempt to tell us that the advertised product can make us glamorous, sexy, successful, or more perfect than we are. One of the products often advertised in this way is cigarettes. This activity will help you analyze these messages.

PART I

SURGEON GENERAL'S WARNING: Quitting Smoking Now Greatly Reduces Serious Risks to Your Health.

Cigarette smoking can help you look older.

If you think smoking adds years to your appearance, remember that it also takes years off your life.

AMERICAN ✝ LUNG ASSOCIATION *of the Southland of Minnesota*

SOURCE: Reprinted by permission of the American Lung Association of Minnesota.

Examine ad number one. What message do you think the cigarette ad is giving? What personal qualities do the two young people in the ad have? Are these positive qualities that you would like to have? Why is there a motorcycle in the ad? Discuss how the ad affects you personally. Do you think it is effective? Would this be a product that you would like to use because of the way it is advertised? Why or why not?

Now look at ad number two. What is its message? How does it contrast with the message in ad number 1? Why is the picture of the skeleton used? Do you think the ad is effective? Discuss how the ad affects you personally. Would this ad change your mind if you were a smoker? Why or why not?

After looking at both ads, decide which message you would pay more attention to. Why?

PART II

Write some factual statements expressed by the messages in the ads.

EXAMPLE: Ad number two suggests that smoking causes disease.

Write some opinionated statements the ads convey.

EXAMPLE: Ad number one suggests that smoking can make you look more cool.

After doing this activity either individually or in small groups, discuss the meanings of the ads in a classroom discussion. How does advertising affect your lives? Do negative advertising messages, like the anti-smoking ad, affect you differently than positive ads? How?

3

PREFACE: Does Smoking Cause Disease?

Many adults smoke, but whether or not they should is a controversial issue. While many people have known someone whose health has been harmed by smoking, many smokers believe this could not happen to them. To complicate the issue, some smokers seem to enjoy good health in spite of their habit.

Nevertheless, many smokers die each year from lung disease, emphysema, and cancer. Much scientific opinion agrees that these diseases are smoking related.

In the next two arguments, you will read the views of two people who have opposing viewpoints on the smoking issue. Viewpoint five is by a free-lance writer and viewpoint six is by The Tobacco Institute. One of the elements that you should take into account when reading opposing viewpoints is what reasons authors may have for their arguments. It is in the interest of The Tobacco Institute, for instance, to sell more cigarettes. You should ask yourself whether this business interest influences its statement. Always ask how authors' personal or professional experiences affect their opinions. Note also that it is possible to have a strong interest in a subject and still present an objective case. This should be something you keep in mind while reading the next two viewpoints.

Look at each argument objectively and use your critical reading and thinking skills. How does each author try to convince you that his opinion is right?

Editor's Note: This viewpoint is paraphrased from an article written by David Owen, a free-lance writer. Mr. Owen argues that there is overwhelming proof that smoking causes disease. He believes that smokers do not accept this fact, however, because of the tobacco companies' attempts to lie to and confuse them. Watch for the facts in both this viewpoint and the next viewpoint. You will find the same facts used, but to make different points.

What facts does the author present in the first paragraph?

The author believes smokers are very interested in what tobacco companies say. Do you think this is a fact or an opinion?

The author gives many examples of why he thinks cigarette companies are powerful. Are all of these examples facts? Why or why not?

Three thousand Americans died of lung cancer in 1930. Today lung cancer kills that many every nine days. The reason for the increase is smoking. In the United States, medical experts believe that smoking is the cause of almost all lung cancer cases and 30 percent of all cancer cases for a total of 350,000 deaths each year.

Tobacco companies argue that these "facts" are not true. Tobacco companies still argue that smoking is not harmful even though there is proof that it is.

Despite this, the cigarette companies are very successful. Tobacco companies sold almost 6 billion cigarettes in 1983.

The success of the "lung cancer industry" proves that the lies spread through cigarette advertising work. Smoking and cancer? "No medical or clinical proof," states Philip Morris, a major tobacco company. The industry's constant lying gives smokers the bit of doubt they need to keep up their habit. Cigarette companies try to make the cancer isssue a "debate," when it is really a scientific fact that smoking causes disease.

The tobacco industry is very powerful. Many groups receive large amounts of money from it. State and federal governments support cigarette companies because of the money the governments make from tobacco sales and export taxes. Magazines and newspapers accept tobacco advertising in order to pay for the cost of printing. Smokers themselves keep the tobacco industry going by continuing to waste their money and health.

Is it really true that smokers freely choose their addiction to cigarettes? Is their "decision" to ruin their health really based on "individual freedom of choice"? The tobacco companies argue that this is true. But it is not. The facts are that more than half of all smokers either do not know or do not believe that smoking causes heart attacks. Forty percent do not know that it causes most lung cancer. Why? Because the tobacco companies spend hundreds of millions of dollars in advertising and public relations so that smokers will keep believing that smoking does not cause disease.

The tobacco industry also spends a lot of money to entrap its customers when they are too young to know any better. Most cigarette advertising is aimed at young people. Marlboro, the most advertised brand, is three times more popular among children and teenagers than it is among adults. If Philip Morris really does not want kids to smoke, why does it use cowboys in its advertising? Why does it plaster its logos on race cars?

Why does the author think smokers continue to smoke? Is this a fact or opinion?

How do tobacco companies stay in business, according to the author? Why do you think kids smoke? Do you think they are too young to know any better?

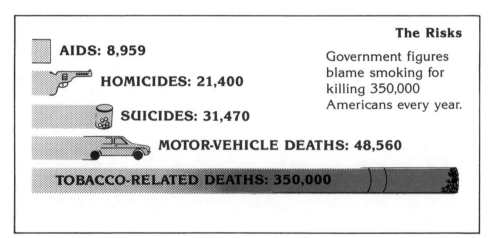

The Risks

AIDS: 8,959

HOMICIDES: 21,400

SUICIDES: 31,470

MOTOR-VEHICLE DEATHS: 48,560

TOBACCO-RELATED DEATHS: 350,000

Government figures blame smoking for killing 350,000 Americans every year.

SOURCE: Centers for Disease Control: 1986 figures

Kids and smoking

List three facts and three opinions the author gives to prove his view that smoking does cause disease.

The author believes that the publications of The Tobacco Institute are harmful. Why? Why does he think The Tobacco Institute makes kids want to smoke? Do you think kids smoke because of the reasons the author gives?

VIEWPOINT 6 Smoking may not cause disease

Editor's Note: The following viewpoint is paraphrased from an article written by Horace R. Kornegay, president of The Tobacco Institute. Mr. Kornegay questions the studies used to prove smoking causes disease. Pay attention to what studies and facts Mr. Kornegay uses to make his case.

What statement about smoking is made in this first paragraph? Is this a fact or opinion?

The author is arguing that the link between smoking and disease is accidental. Does he prove this point?

The author asks a series of questions in order to make us "think." Are any of these questions based on facts?

Many adults smoke because they enjoy it, like you enjoy riding your bike or playing with your friends. But does smoking cause diseases such as cancer and emphysema? No one knows.

The case against smoking is built upon statistics, or numbers that are gathered from studies. But no one has proven without a doubt that these statistics are right. Never before have scientists found a "cause" for as many diseases as they try to pin on smoking.

If smoking causes disease, why do scientists not know how this happens? And why has not a single ingredient been found in cigarettes that produces the diseases?

Statistics are said to show that smokers get sick and die more often than nonsmokers from cancer, heart disease, emphysema, and bronchitis. But the fact that these diseases are more evident at the same time that more people smoke may be just an accident. Just because more smoking and more disease happen at the same time does not mean one causes the other.

Just blaming cigarettes for heart disease does not help. The National Heart and Lung Institute points out that we have learned a lot about treating heart problems, but we still know very little about their causes.

Those people who think smoking is terrible have tried to make the public think so too with these flimsy "facts." But there are other questions the public should think about:

1. Why do most smokers never get the diseases that are supposed to be caused by smoking?

2. Why do nonsmokers sometimes get the same diseases that are caused by smoking? This has to mean that smoking cannot be the only cause of these diseases. In fact, The National Cancer Institute reported that rates for lung cancer among nonsmokers doubled in 1983.

3. Research shows that doctors may be influenced by the fact that their patient smokes. In other words, they may say their patient's illness is caused by smoking, even if it is not.

4. Reports that show the other side of the tobacco issue are ignored by the anti-smoking media. The American Heart Association does not tell us that in Japan, the rates of lung cancer are much lower than in the U.S., even though smoking rates are higher among Japanese men.

Of course, these points do not completely prove that cigarettes do not cause cancer. But it is just as wrong to say that statistics prove cigarettes do cause cancer.

Smoking and health statistics usually compare smokers and nonsmokers. Whenever two groups of people like this are compared, there are many differences. Might there be other differences between these two groups that could explain these health differences? For instance, research shows that smokers are generally more talkative. They are more creative, energetic, and drink more coffee and liquor. And, most importantly, they are more likely to have parents with heart disease and high blood pressure.

> **Why do most smoking studies compare smokers and non-smokers? Why does the author criticize this?**

This last statistic is especially interesting. Scientists know that heredity, characteristics that are passed on from generation to generation, plays a part in personality and some diseases. Might this be true of smokers? Smokers may inherit a tendency toward heart disease, rather than getting it from smoking. This idea is still unexplored.

It is human nature to want to argue something is true when we really do not know. This has been the case among many people who have had something to say about smoking and health.

But true scientists must prove their ideas, and in the case of smoking and health this proof is sorely lacking.

> **Do you think scientists really want to argue about things they do not know about? Do you think the author's statement about human nature is fact or opinion? Why?**

Smoking and disease

List three facts and three opinions the author gives to prove his view that smoking may not cause disease.

The author concludes that scientists simply do not know if smoking causes disease. Do you think that this is true? Why or why not?

3 Understanding Editorial Cartoons

Throughout this book, you have seen cartoons that illustrate the ideas in the viewpoints. Editorial cartoons are an effective and usually humorous way of presenting an opinion on an issue. Cartoonists can place facts as well as opinions in their cartoons. While many cartoons are easy to understand, others may require more thought. The cartoon below deals with the tobacco industry. It is similar to the cartoons that appear in your daily newspaper.

Look at the cartoon. What attitude does the cartoon suggest tobacco companies have about smoking and disease? Do you think the cartoonist agrees or disagrees with the attitude of the tobacco companies? Why?

Don Wright, *Miami News.* Reprinted with permission.

In this book, you have read viewpoints that support the tobacco industry. Do you believe the cartoonist's opinion is accurate? Does the industry ignore overwhelming evidence that smoking is harmful?

For further practice, look at the editorial cartoons in your daily newspaper. Identify the cartoons' opinions. See if you can find a cartoon that uses fact to back up its statement. In a classroom discussion, have you and your class debate whether or not the cartoonist's opinion is one you agree or disagree with.

CHAPTER 4

PREFACE: Would Common Courtesy Solve the Smoking Debate?

In the next two viewpoints, you will find people discussing common courtesy and smoking. Common courtesy means thinking about the people around you, whether they are strangers or friends. You use common courtesy when you are careful not to talk at the movies, or when you let someone go ahead of you at the grocery store. The problem with courtesy, however, is that it may mean different things to different people. The person who talks in the movies probably does not think it is rude. And some people may simply be impolite. Some people just do not care about other people's feelings.

In the smoking debate, some people think smokers should be allowed to smoke only in certain areas of public places, such as restaurants, malls, and government buildings. They want laws that regulate where people can smoke because they do not like breathing cigarette smoke. Some people think smokers are impolite and do not care about how nonsmokers around them feel about their smoke.

Other people believe that nonsmokers are the inconsiderate ones. They think nonsmokers are being selfish by insisting that smoking should not be allowed in some places. They argue that smokers do care about the people around them and do try to use common courtesy about where to smoke. They think that laws restricting smoking will hurt businesses and make smokers angry and unhappy.

The next two viewpoints debate these issues. Pay attention to the facts and opinions each author uses.

Common courtesy can solve the smoking debate

Editor's Note: This viewpoint is paraphrased from a statement published by The Tobacco Institute. The Institute argues that laws restricting smoking in public places are unnecessary. Pay attention to why the writer for the Institute believes this is so. Also, watch for the facts and opinions the Institute uses to support its argument.

What is the reason the author gives for his belief that we do not need anti-smoking laws? Do you think this reason is a fact or opinion? Why?

What kind of people want smoking laws, according to the author? Does he give any facts to support this idea?

Have you heard the one about the airline counter person who asks the passenger whether he would like a seat in the smoking section—or one *inside* the plane?

It may have been funny the first time a comedian told it. But it is really no joke. Smoking laws and regulations are sprouting up all over the country. Now airplanes, jury rooms, restaurants, and offices have no-smoking rules.

How far should government go in controlling personal habits and limiting adult freedom of choice? Most smokers do not need these laws. Most smokers are considerate adults.

Those who argue for smoking laws often say that non-smokers' health is their concern. But these concerns are theories only. The Surgeon General has said that there is not enough proof to argue that other people's smoke affects nonsmokers. The Surgeon General also says no tobacco smoke allergy has been found. He says that what nonsmokers claim is an allergic reaction is really all in their heads.

So, if this is true, then why should government get involved?

We don't think the government *should* get involved. We think people should work out solutions to the smoking problem.

Dr. Theodore Gill has written that these kinds of laws do not work. They are forced on us by people who look to government to solve their arguments.

He added that in touchy areas such as smoking, that involve personal taste, "common courtesy should prevail."

Dr. Gill is right. Do we really need police officers checking smoking in restaurants, on airplanes, and in offices? Of course not.

Business owners do not need smoking laws. They will work out the problems between smokers and nonsmokers privately.

In fact, some business owners believe such laws could put them out of business. As an owner of a California restaurant said, "If they came in and told me I could allow smoking in only one section, and nonsmoking in another . . . I couldn't operate."

The police do not want smoking laws either. "We've got enough problems catching burglars," was the way Undersheriff Tom Rosa of California put it.

Smokers and nonsmokers, we hope, will continue living and working together as they have for years, without laws. They know that life is a matter of give and take.

And a smoker knows when it is OK to light up. Most are polite enough to stop on their own when it is obvious that they might bother others.

Common sense tells us not to raise our voices in a restaurant or a busy office. It tells us not to bathe in heavy perfume or overdo the garlic before going to the movies.

Common sense tells us that cooperation and mutual understanding are the simplest means by which smokers and nonsmokers can get along.

Common sense is for the common good, like the Golden Rule. And it might even make sure that no one will ever have to ride *outside* the plane.

The author uses quotes from one business owner and one police officer to support his argument. Are these quotes fact or opinion?

Is the author's point about common sense a fact or an opinion? Why?

What point is the author making in this final paragraph? Is it based on a fact or on an opinion?

Is common courtesy enough?

Can you list at least three facts the authors give to prove their view that smoking laws are not needed?

Can you list at least three opinions?

What do the authors conclude about common courtesy? Do you think this is right? Have you ever been in the school restroom or in the non-smoking section of a restaurant with your family when someone starts to smoke? What happens? Does your answer match the authors' view that "common courtesy" is followed? Do you find the authors' argument convincing? Why or why not?

Common courtesy cannot solve the smoking debate

Editor's Note: This viewpoint is paraphrased from a newspaper column by Ellen Goodman. Throughout the article, she criticizes an ad published by a major tobacco company. She believes that public smoking laws are needed. Read carefully for the facts and opinions Ms. Goodman uses to back her viewpoint.

"THEY DON'T LOOK LIKE PASSIVE SMOKERS TO ME...."

Reprinted by permission.

Is the author's dialogue more or less realistic than the one in the Reynolds ad? Why or why not?

Isn't it wonderful, theater lovers? The R.J. Reynolds company, which for so many years has been writing fiction into its cigarette ads, is now writing plays.

Its very first attempt is a charming tale on the subject of smoking and common courtesy. It is being printed in magazines in the latest series of public-image advertising.

The R.J. Reynolds Company begins the ad by explaining its motives. We are told, "These days the level of social talk between smokers and nonsmokers is approaching that of a tag-team wrestling match." Their "daring solution: greater courtesy . . ."

On the center stage are two main characters. One, a male smoker, is about to light a cigarette. He is seated next to a female nonsmoker. Here is the dialogue:

HE: "Excuse me, do you mind if I smoke?"

SHE: "I don't mind as long as you don't let your smoke blow in my face."

HE: "I'll do my best. Let me know if the smoke bothers you."

SHE: "I will and thanks for asking."

HE: "Thanks for being so understanding."

That's it. The curtain goes down to thunderous applause. The narrator concludes: "Common courtesy. It's just crazy enough, it might work."

Now, mind you, the dialogue that I have quoted above is not up for a Tony Award. The stakes are much, much higher than that. The tobacco people are fighting for air space.

The same scene in real life is not necessarily like the one in Reynolds' road show. The same encounter may sound more like this:

SMOKER: "Excuse me, do you mind if I smoke?"

NONSMOKER: "Yes, I do mind."

The nonsmokers have stopped believing that they have to breathe in someone else's bad habit. Smoking is becoming as unacceptable as spitting.

The tobacco companies—which do not fear lung cancer, emphysema, or heart disease—are afraid of public pressure. They portray the nonsmoker as a rude radical. The tobacco people are then seen as the voice of reason. The nonsmokers are asked to "understand."

Well, forgive me for being rude, but "understanding" the smoker sharing your air is a bit like giving someone permission to stand on your feet. It is important to keep the characters straight. The smoker is the aggressor. The nonsmoker is the defender.

But back to the courtesy charade. One of the great lines in this ad did not even make the dialogue. It is a stage footnote:

"We continue to believe in the power of politeness to change the world." So do I. Over the years I have tried asking the cigarette companies if they would stop directing their advertising to young people. Please. I have asked them if they would stop pretending that cigarettes did not cause lung cancer. Pretty please. I have even, ever so nicely, suggested that they should stop selling a product that is clearly deadly.

To be frank, I do not think that it is civil to sell lung cancer. Nor is it courteous to produce heart disease. It must surely be impolite to be responsible for 350,000 cigarette-related deaths a year.

I would like to read a little play about people who push cigarettes all day and how they sleep at night. Maybe if I asked them nicely, they would write one. After all, we nonsmokers have to watch our manners these days. I will say, "Pretty, pretty please with sugar on top."

What point is the author making in this paragraph? Is she using fact or opinion?

What does the author compare "understanding the smoker" to? Is her point based on fact or opinion? How can you tell?

Source: Michael Keefe for the *Denver Post*, reprinted with permission.

What are the facts the author uses in this paragraph?

A ridiculous idea?

List three facts and three opinions the author gives to prove her view that common courtesy is not going to work.

The author thinks the issue of common courtesy is ridiculous. Why? Give a reason you think that common courtesy might work to solve the smoking debate. Give a reason you think that it would not work.

CRITICAL THINKING SKILL 4

Distinguishing Between Fact and Opinion

This activity will allow you to practice distinguishing between fact and opinion. The statements below focus on the subject matter of this chapter, whether common courtesy can solve the smoking debate. Read each statement and consider it carefully. *Mark O for any statement you believe is an opinion, or what one person believes to be true. Mark F for any statement you believe is a fact, or something that can be proven to be true. Mark U for any statement for which you cannot decide.*

If you are doing this activity as a member of a class or group, compare your answers with other class or group members. You will find that others may have different answers than you do. Listening to the reasons others give for their answers can help you in distinguishing fact from opinion.

EXAMPLE: The government should not have laws telling people where they can smoke.

ANSWER: Opinion: this statement expresses one person's opinion. Others would disagree.

Answer

1. All people are courteous and polite, when given a chance. _____

2. Just because we have laws against smoking does not mean that everyone will obey the laws. _____

3. The Surgeon General says that passive smoking is dangerous. _____

4. The power of politeness can change the world. _____

5. Nonsmokers shouldn't have to breathe in someone else's bad habit. _____

6. There are 350,000 cigarette-related deaths each year. _____

7. Most people will put out a cigarette if they are asked politely. _____

8. There are many laws which regulate smoking in public places. _____

9. Northwest Orient banned smoking on all less-than two hour flights. This was the worst idea in history. _____